LIVING SPARKS OF GOD

Stories of Saints for Young Catholics to Color

Maria and Michael LaVoy

29 28 27 26 25 4 5 6 7 8 9 10

ISBN: 978-1-68192-520-2
RELIGION / Christianity / Catholic
LCCN: 2019939969

Design and typesetting: Jerry Windley-Daoust

Printed in the United States of America

Michael LaVoy does art at www.genoneart.com

All living creatures are sparks
from the radiance of God's brilliance,
and these sparks emerge from God
like the rays of the sun.
—St. Hildegard of Bingen

Dedication
For our children and godchildren.

Cut along the outside edge of each illustration
to create an 8" × 10" artwork suitable for framing.

Saint Joseph

Jesus looked up at him. No words needed to be spoken. In the silence, they understood one another. As Jesus waited for Joseph's approval, Joseph chuckled to himself. He didn't doubt that one day the student would surpass the teacher! It was clear the skills of Joseph's trade came naturally to Jesus.

"Your mother will love it!" Joseph said with great affection. As the earthy smell of wood shavings filled the air, Joseph thought about how much he treasured the simple time they got to spend working alongside one another, perhaps even more now. Was it already a month ago when he and Mary had been filled with such great anxiety as they searched for Jesus in Jerusalem? Joseph's heart tightened as he thought about the fear he and Mary had felt when they couldn't find him.

A sudden stab of pain shot through Joseph's finger.

"I'm so sorry, Father!" Jesus exclaimed.

"Don't worry, Jesus . . . my finger and the hammer are not strangers. They have met many times before!" Joseph laughed and tousled Jesus' hair. "But what do you say we take a break for lunch?"

More to the story!

We don't know much about Joseph, but we do know he was a just and pious man whose ancestor was King David, the most important king in Jewish history. Joseph was also a carpenter, a trade that didn't make him rich, but kept his family comfortable. Joseph loved Jesus greatly and cared for his safety.

Saints Perpetua and Felicity

The guard roughly shoved the young women into the prison. Perpetua helped Felicity up. At eight months pregnant, Felicity was weak from the suffocating heat of the overcrowded prison. The heat and darkness of the prison were hard on Perpetua, too, but most agonizing was being separated from her precious baby boy. Little did she know, however, that her anxiety would soon be lifted.

The moment that Perpetua's son was brought to her felt heavenly! Her prison seemed to transform into a palace as she held her baby in her arms again. It was the medicine Perpetua needed to regain her strength, and it was this strength that helped Felicity give birth to a beautiful baby girl just two days before she and Perpetua were to be executed.

Even though death would soon separate them from their children, Perpetua and Felicity trusted God. Both women had been given the gift of a mother's love, and their gift helped them understand their Heavenly Father's love for them. It was his love and power that would give them the strength to joyfully face death in the arena, surrounded by wild beasts.

More to the story!

Saints Perpetua and Felicity were arrested and sentenced to death for their decision to become Christian at a time when Christians were being persecuted by Emperor Septimius Severus. God's goodness ordered that Perpetua and Felicity's children were cared for after their death.

Saint Marcellus the Centurion

The grand birthday festival of Emperor Maximian was in full swing. Sounds of lively music and the scent of exotic spices filled the air. Everyone was celebrating. Everyone, that is, except Marcellus. As a Roman soldier, Marcellus was expected to participate, but he simply couldn't join the others in their extravagant feasting and sinful sacrificing. The pressure to join in was great, but Marcellus's newfound faith was even stronger.

Marcellus took his vine staff, the stick that symbolized his military status, and threw it down. "I am a soldier of Jesus Christ, the Eternal King, and I can serve no other!" he boldly declared. He also surrendered his military belt and arms. His voice rose even louder, "If, as a man of service, I am forced to offer sacrifice to gods and emperors, then I refuse to serve!" His fellow soldiers stood in shock at Marcellus' offensive words and actions. When a few regained their senses, they roughly grabbed hold of Marcellus and reported him to the commander of the legion, who had Marcellus immediately thrown into prison. Surely madness had overtaken Marcellus! He would come to his senses once the festival was over!

More to the story!

When the festival had ended, Marcellus was given the opportunity to renounce his words and actions, but he again declared his Christianity. Death by the sword was his sentence, but the victory of martyrdom was his reward.

Blessed Jacoba de Settesoli

Francis was dying, and he wanted his good friend to be at his side. He asked one of his brothers to write a letter to Lady Jacoba, telling her to come without delay. She must bring some cloth for a tunic . . . and also the sweet confection she had made for him when he visited her in Rome.

No sooner had the letter been written when there was a knock on the door. It was Lady Jacoba! But how could it be? The letter hadn't even been sent yet! Nonetheless, there she stood, holding the gray cloth for the tunic. She had even brought the ingredients for those delicious treats!

A brother brought Lady Jacoba to where Francis lay dying. Tears filled her eyes at the sight of her cherished friend. Then she explained how she had arrived so quickly. "While I was praying," she said, "a voice within told me I urgently needed to visit my father, blessed Francis, and everything I should bring with me."

Soon after, Jacoba set to work making her famous puffed pastries. The scent of honey, cream, and almonds filled the air. Although he was only able to eat a little, Francis savored one last taste of his favorite treat . . . and his sweet friendship with Lady Jacoba.

More to the story!

Jacoba de Settesoli was a friend and follower of St. Francis of Assisi, who often visited her in Rome. He taught her that her acts of self-sacrifice as a wife and mother were her path to holiness.

Saint Juan Diego

Juan Diego couldn't meet the beautiful Lady again today. There simply was no time. She would understand that his uncle was dying and that Juan desperately needed to get a priest!

Besides, he had already told the Noble Lady he didn't feel that he was the man for the job. Twice Juan had gone to the bishop to make known her request to have a church built on top of Tepeyac hill, and twice the bishop didn't believe him. And now the bishop wanted a sign to prove that Juan's message really came from Mary, mother of the True God!

All of these remarkable happenings filled Juan's head as he hurried along a different path—one that avoided the top of the hill where the Blessed Virgin had appeared to him. Then, suddenly, the Lady was before him! His cheeks grew fiery red with embarrassment. With a tender sweetness, Mary assured him his uncle would get well, and instructed him to go to the top of the hill.

To Juan's amazement, there he found stunning, fragrant roses where roses never grew—and in winter! He picked some, placed them in his tilma, and carried them back to the Lady. As she arranged the flowers, Mary told him, "These are the sign that you are to give the Bishop."

More to the story!

When Juan Diego brought the roses to the bishop, they fell to the ground, and a miraculous image of the Lady was revealed on Juan's tilma. A church was built where the Lady appeared, and millions converted to Christianity.

Saint Martin de Porres

He couldn't keep the other brothers from poisoning them much longer. Martin stopped sweeping and headed to the monastery's wardrobe room. He knew the others didn't share his affection for the little creatures. True, they were eating holes in the monks' robes, but there had to be a way to solve the dilemma without killing the mice.

As Martin entered the room, he spied one of his little friends and gently scooped him up. Peering down at the wide-eyed mouse, Martin noticed a hole in the sleeve of his own habit that needed mending. He chuckled to himself. Here he was about to explain to the little mouse that chewing holes in the fine linen robes was causing harm, even though he didn't mind the holes in his own worn-out habit!

Nevertheless, for the sake of the others, Martin told the mouse to gather all his little friends and guide them outside, to the far end of the monastery garden. Martin added that he would feed them every day if they never again touched the wardrobe. Then, he kindly set the mouse down. Without delay, all the other mice scurried from their hiding places and made their way to the garden. Martin himself led the mouse parade, and both he and the mice kept their agreement from that day forward!

More to the story!

St. Martin de Porres loved animals and seemed to have the amazing gift of being able to talk with them. He is also known for the many miracles that happened when he was serving the poor and sick.

Saint Kateri Tekakwitha

Tekakwitha must marry," her uncle angrily said to his wife, "but those Blackrobes have filled her head with silly ideas of chastity and purity!"

Kateri winced as she overheard her uncle's words from inside their longhouse. He didn't understand that she was not her own. She had given herself to Jesus, and he must be her only love. In fact, it was clear no one understood her refusal to marry. Not only was she being punished with more work, but the other girls had stopped talking to her. Wrapping herself in a blanket, Kateri snuck out of the longhouse and headed to her favorite spot along the water's edge.

There, as she sat listening to the water flowing over the rocks, she recalled the day she took her new baptismal name, Kateri. How great was the love of God that she had felt that day! She knew she was an example of this love, even to those who treated her like a slave; however, her life was now in danger. Even though her uncle would never allow it, Kateri realized she had to leave her home.

More to the story!

When Kateri was very young, she became sick with a disease called smallpox. The disease left her an orphan with very poor eyesight and a badly scarred face. Those in her new home, the Mission of St. Francis Xavier, said that after she died, the scars on her face completely disappeared, and her face shone with radiant beauty.

Saint Dominic Savio

The boy's blood boiled as he prepared to fight his opponent. He held a sharp, heavy stone in one hand, as did the other boy . . . the scoundel who had insulted his family! He couldn't wait to hurl his rock and split open the other boy's head.

But now their good friend Dominic stepped between the two boys. What did Dominic think he was doing? He had already tried to stop the fight once, but the boys had refused to listen.

"Before the fight begins, I have one condition you must follow," Dominic declared with great conviction, "Do you promise?"

"If it gets you out of our way, yes!" the first boy shouted impatiently. The other also agreed to follow Dominic's condition.

Dominic held up a crucifix. "Look at this crucifix and say, 'Jesus was innocent and He died forgiving those who hated him rather than seeking vengeance!'"

Then Dominic walked over to the first boy and said, "Now, throw the first stone at me!"

"Why would I do that? You are my friend!" the boy replied, shaken.

Dominic ran to the other angry boy and demanded the same thing.

"Never!" cried the other boy.

"Why would you want to hurt God and not me?" Dominic asked them.

The boy's stone dropped from his hand. An icy chill ran down his spine. He hated himself. He had been willing to commit a sin instead of forgiving, and Dominic's heroic action had saved him from making a grave error.

More to the story!

St. Dominic attended the Oratory of St. Francis de Sales run by St. Don Bosco. This incident is one of many in which he modeled great virtue and demonstrated his motto, "Death, but not sin!"

IN
RI

Saint Bernadette Soubirous

Bernadette stood shivering at the edge of the icy stream. Toinette and Jeanne had already splashed across to collect firewood in the grotto, but Bernadette wasn't eager to join her sister and friend. Reluctantly, she started taking off her stockings.

The sound of a great, rushing wind caused her to look up. There, in a small opening in the grotto, Bernadette saw a beautiful, radiant Lady dressed in white, with a blue sash around her waist and golden roses at her feet!

The Lady smiled, and the fear Bernadette had felt immediately left her. When Bernadette saw the white and gold rosary that hung on the Lady's arm, she instinctively grabbed her own rosary and started to pray. As she did, the Lady silently passed the beads of her rosary between her fingers, speaking only to say each Gloria with Bernadette. Her voice was so sweet to Bernadette's ears!

When the prayer was finished, the Lady vanished as mysteriously as she had come, leaving Bernadette kneeling in complete elation.

More to the story!

This was the first of eighteen appearances of the Virgin Mary to fourteen-year-old Bernadette. Identifying herself as the Immaculate Conception, the Lady showed Bernadette a miraculous spring of water, near which a chapel was eventually built.

Saint John Bosco

"Quick, quick!" the boy yelled to his friend, "you have to come see John Bosco!" Together the boys ran up to the crowd and made their way to the front.

The boy, who had seen John before, bubbled over with excitement. "Watch what he is going to do next!"

The words of the dream echoed inside John's head as he stepped out onto the tightrope: "This is the field of your work. Be humble, steadfast, and strong!" After taking one more glance at the captivated audience of young boys, not much younger than himself, John stretched out his arms and charmingly made his way to the center of the rope.

Once in position, he juggled his set of colored balls, rhythmically tossing them in the air and catching them. Then he walked the remainder of the rope and ended his act.

The joy-filled audience burst into energetic applause. When the excitement had died down, John did what he always did at the end of his act. Instead of passing around his hat to collect money, he invited his new friends to come with him to Mass.

More to the story!

When John was a boy, he had a powerful dream that positively set him on the path of his life's work: saving souls, especially those of poor and neglected young boys.

IHS

Saint Thérèse of Lisieux

Thérèse could barely contain her excitement! She and her family had just returned from Midnight Mass, and now Thérèse was eagerly looking forward to finding sweet Christmas treats and presents in the "magic shoes" she had left by the fireplace! Oh, how she would delight in each surprise!

Her Papa, on the other hand, didn't share in her excitement; it was late, and he was tired. "Well, fortunately, this will be the last year!" she overheard him say in annoyance as he passed her shoes.

The words sharply pierced her oversensitive heart, and the tears immediately began to glisten in Thérèse's eyes.

Then, in a single, extraordinary moment, something changed. By God's grace, Thérèse felt charity enter her soul, and the need to forget herself in order to please others. No longer the same, she merrily bounded down the stairs and joyfully opened her presents. Her father even recovered his own cheerfulness. Her sister Céline felt like it was all a dream! Had Thérèse really overcome her hurt without making a scene and bursting into tears like she always had before? Was the source of so many tears she had cried in her childhood really dried up? Indeed they were, and from that moment on, Thérèse's spiritual life began to truly blossom.

More to the story!

Thérèse calls this event the grace of her complete conversion. Although, she went on to live a simple, short life as a Carmelite nun, she became very well-known for the spirituality of her Little Way and is recognized as a Doctor of the Church.

INRI

Blessed Pier Giorgio Frassati

He had exactly one hour, but he wasn't worried. Antonio needed Pier Giorgio's bus fare money more than he did. Besides, he needed to keep up his training if he was going to go climbing in the Val di Lanzo in a few weeks. If he chose his course wisely, and ran fast enough, he would have enough time to stop and pray before his Lord in the Blessed Sacrament and still be home in time for dinner!

Pushing up and off the pavement, Pier Giorgio quickly settled into a short, quick stride. His mind drifted to the families he had visited that day. In just a little time, how much good he could do for those he visited, and how much good he could do for himself! As he approached his favorite hill, he reflected on how being a member of the St. Vincent De Paul Society was an amazing way he could help serve the poor that he cared so deeply about. Keeping his head up and looking straight ahead, Pier Giorgio sprinted even faster up the hill. It was nothing compared to the mountains he climbed, but still, it reminded him of his purpose, and the reason he served Turin's sick and needy: to keep striving toward the top!

More to the story!

During his short life, Blessed Pier Giorgio was an avid mountain climber who spent his free time helping the poor. He also liked to go to daily Mass with his friends. His daily life reflected the name given to him by St. Pope John Paul II, "The Man of the Eight Beatitudes."

Blessed Miguel Pro

Excuse me good sir, could you spare a poor beggar some bread?" Quickly, Padre Pro was ushered inside and upstairs to the room where the baby waited. Safely inside, he removed his tattered disguise and warmly greeted the others in the room. Despite their fear, they couldn't help but feel joyful now that he was here. The Padre looked at the precious bundle held in the arms of her godmother. "What do you ask of the Church of God?" Padre Pro began. Then he went on to baptize little Maria Esperanza.

After the ceremony, the family thanked Padre Pro by treating him to some fresh cocol. They knew him too well. He couldn't pass up his favorite childhood treat! After sharing some laughter, Padre announced it was time for him to go.

"But Padre Miguel, aren't you afraid?" asked little José.

"Why should I be? I always carry arms." Padre Pro pulled a small crucifix out from under his shirt. "These are my arms," he said with a wink. "With this I am afraid of nothing." Then, he slipped quietly back into the night.

More to the story!

Blessed Miguel Pro was a Jesuit priest during a time of severe Catholic persecution in Mexico. As a result, he had to meet people's spiritual needs in secret. Eventually, he was captured and sentenced to death; his last words were, "*Viva Cristo Rey!*" Long live Christ the King!

Blessed Chiara Luce Badano

"I was standing behind my baseline and had just called out the score, 'Love-all.' Then, I tossed the ball up and started my swing motion, and that's when I first felt it."

Chiara and her parents were sitting in the doctor's office, waiting for the results of tests he had ordered. Chiara was telling them again about the first time she felt the very sharp pain in her shoulder. She wanted to reassure her parents (and herself) that she had just injured her shoulder playing tennis, but somehow she knew it was more serious.

Her doctor walked in, and his somber look said it all. Osteogenic sarcoma, a serious and painful form of cancer, was the diagnosis. Chiara could feel her heart quicken and her stomach drop. The devastating news was almost too much for the lively teenager to think about.

At first, Chiara struggled with the weight of her sorrow. But in the end, she was able to declare, "For you, Jesus! If you want it, I want it too!"

From that moment on, she joyfully allowed God to reward her with love, and she chose to truly "love all," even her suffering.

More to the story!

Blessed Chiara Luce went on to fight cancer bravely. Her joy increased with her suffering because she was able to offer her suffering to Jesus. Right before she died, she said, "Be happy, because I'm happy."

INRI
salumeria
AMARETTI SASSELO
CAFFE' TUBINO